Anke Werckmeister

Femininity and Masculinity Constructions in "Alfie"

GRIN Verlag

Bibliografische Information der Deutschen Nationalbibliothek:

Die Deutsche Bibliothek verzeichnet diese Publikation in der Deutschen National-
bibliografie; detaillierte bibliografische Daten sind im Internet über http://dnb.d-
nb.de/ abrufbar.

Imprint:

Copyright © 2007 GRIN Verlag GmbH
Druck und Bindung: Books on Demand GmbH, Norderstedt Germany
ISBN: 978-3-656-29434-4

This book at GRIN:

http://www.grin.com/en/e-book/202923/femininity-and-masculinity-constructions-
in-alfie

GRIN - Your knowledge has value

Der GRIN Verlag publiziert seit 1998 wissenschaftliche Arbeiten von Studenten, Hochschullehrern und anderen Akademikern als eBook und gedrucktes Buch. Die Verlagswebsite www.grin.com ist die ideale Plattform zur Veröffentlichung von Hausarbeiten, Abschlussarbeiten, wissenschaftlichen Aufsätzen, Dissertationen und Fachbüchern.

Visit us on the internet:

http://www.grin.com/

http://www.facebook.com/grincom

http://www.twitter.com/grin_com

Freie Universität Berlin
Institut für Englische Philologie
VS Culture, Gender, Media II: Sex and Gender in Sixties Britain

'Femininity and Masculinity Constructions in Alfie'

Anke Werckmeister

August 21st, 2007

1

Contents

Introduction   page 3

I.   Femininity   page 3

1.   Showstoppers   page 3

1.1. Dori   page 3

1.2. Julie   page 4

1.3. Liz   page 5

1.4. Lonette   page 6

2.   Quickies   page 7

2.1. Uta and Carol   page 7

2.2. Lesbians   page 7

2.3. Nikki   page 8

II. Masculinity   page 9

1.   Alfie and the minor characters   page 9

1.1. Alfie   page 9

1.2. Marlon   page 11

1.3. Mr. Wing   page 11

Conclusion   page 12

Cited Works   page 13

Introduction

The 2004 remake of the 1966 original *Alfie* movie once again introduces a charmed, vain, rakish, and women-loving man to our screen. The story itself has not changed much and *Alfie* is still one of the best women-devouring men around New York City this time, so that makes it interesting for us to talk about femininity as well as masculinity since there are so many different types of women involved with *Alfie*. The gender construction here is very interesting to explore more deeply and how it affects the male lead and protagonist *Alfie*. So I want to argue that from the very first scene, because of the construction of it, each and every woman *Alfie* interacts with we can already guess how that particular female character is constructed in terms of femininity and we can also guess how it will affect *Alfie* and his decisions.

I. Femininity

1. Showstoppers

A showstopper, as *Alfie* calls them, is the perfect woman with the perfect body and figure who functions the way *Alfie* wants her to. She then, of course, must fit into his F.B.B. measurement, which is face-boobs-bum, if that does not convince him he will not consider her for a lay. She should also be superficial enough to be one of his showstoppers, but not only that counts for him. The most important thing for *Alfie* is still having sex - promiscuous sex. No matter if it is a sexually neglected married woman, a single mother/housewife, a rich elderly woman, or his best friend's girl.

1.1. Dori

The first of his showstoppers we meet is Dori. A sexually depressed woman who is married to a businessman, Phil, who at that point of the movie, has not laid her for six months. No wonder a sexually depressed and neglected woman seeks *Alfie*'s help in terms of having sex. The picture we get of her in her very first scene is that she fits into *Alfie*'s F.B.B. measurement. A beautiful, sexy face, Dori is a blonde with a voluptuous and breathtaking figure who obviously likes having sex in the car. Moans is the only thing the audience get to know and then there is a cut to not only hear but also see them act in the back of *Alfie*'s limosine. A provocative, half-naked woman sitting on *Alfie*'s lap and he is talking to the camera as if this would be a normal thing to do in that situation. Here one can

3

clearly see that since they have sex in the car and have been doing that for quite a few times that Dori is the one-night-stand person for *Alfie*. Due to her marriage to Phil, they cannot go to Dori's place and since *Alfie* hardly ever takes home his girls they need to do it in his car, which is an indicator that it will not last for a long time.

That is the one and only sex scene they have in the movie; after that *Alfie* has flings with other women. Only when the love of his life breaks his heart and throws away the flowers he bought to propose to her is when Dori and *Alfie* meet again. She appears to be disappointed, even a little hurt, that he did not ring through in the meantime but she knew it from the beginning. And even though she was "quite a number", as *Alfie* says, she was only one of many he slept with. That furthermore is her strongest moment in the film when she tells him that she does not want to see him again because she feels used and exploited at that point.

1.2. Julie

Julie is a single mother who is presented as a housewife in her first scene. The very first we get to see of her is when she is looking through the window hoping to see *Alfie* coming home. Julie is a dark haired woman, slim, tall, not particularly presented as sexy and seductive, but rather motherly and caring. She is in the kitchen preparing the food for *Alfie* and does not appear to be waiting to be taken. She is dressed in a pair of blue jeans and a jersey, so she does not seem to care for her looks.

What she does not know at that point is that she only functions "as his back-up girlfriend" as Desson Thomson suggests (http://www.washingtonpost.com/wp-dyn/content/article/2004/11/05/AR2005033112665.html). *Alfie* just comes home from a one-night-stand with Dori that she does not know about yet and only wants to eat and sleep. And when Julie tries to seduce him on the couch he says his cassette is unloaded and that he wants to sleep. Later on when she tells him that she loves him- an uncommon thing for Alfie to hear- he only replies with a "thanks". Susan Brownmiller says that especially for women love is important which, for Julie, is absolutely true.

> "A requirement of femininity is that a woman devote her life to love- to mother love, to romantic love, to religious love, amorphous, undifferentiated caring." (215)

As Brownmiller goes on arguing, "the point is feeling" and Julie feels love for Alfie but he as a man does not have the same feeling for her because he only comes back to her when he feels like he needs a home and a family, which proves that he does not love her (215). Julie is terribly upset and starts arguing that he would not love her, which is indeed

4

true, but he does not admit it yet. As Joshua Tyler says Julie "feeds his nurturing side. A single mother, she provides for him a family environment he can slip in and out of, like a snake shedding its skin" (http://www.cinemablend.com/reviews/Alfie-714.html). He is absolutely right, *Alfie* only uses Julie to give him the feeling that he is needed as a father. A sentimental side of him that *Alfie* reveals when we meet Julie's little son in the same scene. He advises to never fall in love with a single mom because she has got something irresistible which is the child.

She furthermore thinks that she is only his booty call because he uses her as he wants to and when he needs to; but when she wants him he is tired. She is probably not superficial enough to satisfy his needs for a showstopper. *Alfie* says she is cute and adorable but he wonders if she can be superficial enough to make him stay with her. Obviously she cannot. She leaves him and finds someone new. Later when they meet again she is much more self-confident and radiates sexyness as if now that she is rid of *Alfie* she is a new person.

1.3. Liz

Another of *Alfie*'s showstoppers is the rich, elderly, red-haired Liz. He assumes she is fifty but he says that fifty is the new forty and it immediately clicks between them. In the first scene Liz is presented in a fur coat sitting in the back of his limosine. There she already radiates her self-assurance, sexyness, experience with men and knowledge of them. Liz furthermore shows that older women can be interesting and sexually attractive, even to younger men, and she is very self-assured about her sexual allurements; so she gives the camera a very seductive look. In the next scene we see her in a short tight black dress covering her voluptuous and attractive body which makes *Alfie* go crazy because she emphazises her sexyness even more with her outfit. But when he comes closer to her seeing her revealing cleavage and ample bosom he finds a tattoo on her left breast that excites him enormously. He has never seen a woman like Liz before with her blossoming femininity. That inspires him to have a fling with her but *Alfie* does not realize yet that she only wants him to be her toyboy to satisfy her sexual needs. Her drug abuse and alcohol consumption not only impresses him but also leads him into doing the same which makes her look like a bike chick.

Liz is obviously a sexual-orientated woman who does not care for the love of her men. She wants to be admired for her looks, her beauty and seeks confirmation through having a lot of sex. The more men she can have and seduce, the more self-assured she will be. Liz had all the men she needed in her life when she was younger that is why she wants to have fun now, enjoy her life and does not want to get hooked on anyone because a steady boyfriend would disturb her life. And so Liz does not care for *Alfie*'s feeling when he vistis her to propose to her and instead finds another man with her. She only says that he is younger than *Alfie* when he wants to know what the man in the bathroom has what he does not have. "He is younger than you are" explicitly tells us that she was out for a toyboy from the start and it shows her unpredictability towards men. She never had any feelings for *Alfie* and never said she loved him which was also an indicator that she never wanted more than sex.

1.4. Lonette

Lonette is the next of *Alfie*'s showstoppers with the best bum *Alfie* has ever seen,the of course, she fits perfectly into his F.B.B. measurement. Lonette dated *Alfie*'s best friend Marlon, whom she was seperated from, and *Alfie* was supposed to help Marlon to get back to Lonette. What we get to see of Lonette in her first scene is a close-up on her bum which shakes a bit because she walks through her bar. She is African-American, one thing that changed in the remake, wearing a very short and tight sexy black dress showing lots of cleavage and a chain dangling from her breasts. She radiates a sexyness no man could ever possibly resist. To *Alfie* she is exciting and seductive when playing pool billard and there is something in the air that spills her sex appeal to the audience.

From the audience point of view, one can argue that they will not only end up having sex but also that she will get pregnant. As we know men first look at a woman's bum which for men instinctively tells them how they will fit their needs for giving birth for their children. The broader the hips, the better it is for giving birth. The movie plays with that fact and builds Lonette's story upon it. Even though *Alfie* did not get to see her bum first, as the audience did, but still he ended up with Lonette. Indeed, Lonette dances very seductively next to the jukebox while playing pool with *Alfie* and she persistently asks him why he has never shown any interest in her and if she had done anything wrong in the past that he would not want her. The more she dances, the more *Alfie*'s gaze is focused on her body. Linda Williams says that in that case there is an "encroaching power of visual sexuality" which is true for Alfie because at that moment he already thinks about making love to Lonette (22). Her body language addressing *Alfie* more than just signals that she wants him after her "fertility dance". Elizabeth Grosz also implies that bodies speak a language to give other people signals:

"Bodies speak, without necessarily talking, because they become coded with and as signs. They speak social codes. They become intextuated, narrativized." (35)

The effect of that is that they make love on the pool table and the result of it is that Lonette is pregnant. At first she decides to have an abortion but after coming from the doctor's she feels empty and the audience do not know if she had it aborted or not. As we can see later in the movie she did get his child. When *Alfie* visits her and Marlon in the countryside she seems upset and scared because she did not tell *Alfie* about their child. That is a point in the film when she needs to be very strong, she also wants to maintain her composure but Lonette as well as *Alfie* get emotional and at the same time she seems to be relieved that *Alfie* finally knows the truth. But Lonette knew from the beginning that it would not be serious with him and so it was better for both of them not to get too much involved.

2. Quickies

The women *Alfie* chooses to meet once or twice only also fit into his F.B.B. measurement which is for him the best index to find the most suitable woman for him. No matter if blond, brunette, or black haired he loves them all and they love him and he does not care if they are heterosexual or homosexual. *Alfie* is available for each and every woman.

2.1. Uta and Carol

Uta is one of the few seen women in the movie as well as Carol. Carol only has one line and when she says hello to *Alfie* he does not even remember her because it was so terrible with her. She is a brunette, slim, tall and feminine, but she is dressed boyish-like and rather unsexy. Uta, on the contrary, is black-haired, always elegantly dresses, also slim and sexy, but very beautiful at the same time and certainly *Alfie*'s type. But the only problem he has got when sitting in the bathtub with Uta is that he suddenly is impotent. Even though she is presented as very seductive sitting in the bathtub playing with the bubble bath and trying to seduce *Alfie* he stays impotent. But since he cannot do it with her she is understandably very irritated and angry at him. And that is the last we see of Uta in the movie.

2.2. Lesbians

Two other women we see *Alfie* with are blondes who are very attractive in short tiny dresses whose names are not mentioned because they are rather minor characters. The two

7

of them are very feminine and they also play with their feminine sexuality while they kiss each other in front of *Alfie* in order to turn him on. The audience do not get to know if they are real lesbians or if they only kiss to get *Alfie* into their bed. Maybe they only construct their identity as lesbians because it fits the situation.

> "Inasmuch as "identity" is assured through the stabilizing concepts of sex, gender, and sexuality, the very notion of "the person" is called into question by the cultural emergence of those "incoherent" or "discontinuous" gendered beings who appear to be persons but who fail to conform to the gendered norms of cultural intelligibility by which persons are defined." (Judith Butler, 23)

Here the girls fail to the gendered norms of being heterosexual and instead they define themselves as homosexuals for the possibility of having sex. In the next scene we see them again with *Alfie* and they are trying to have sex but *Alfie* has to pass again because he still has trouble getting an erection; so we only see the girls kissing and touching themselves and then they disappear behind the couch.

2.3. Nikki

One of *Alfie*'s next girls, is the Christmas Angel, Nikki, whom he meets on Christmas Eve. She is, at first sight, a smoking, drug-addicted Hippie girl, at least she is dressed like one but in a modern way. Nikki is a freckled, blond, small, sexy, girlish-looking woman wearing a short miniskirt, overknee boots and a tight fur encrusted jacket which makes her look very attractive to *Alfie*. Her sex appeal radiates so much that Alfie kisses her right away in their first scene even though he only got to know her. That appearance already tells the audience that *Alfie* is out for a fling only. As Rebecca Murray suggests "there's definitely more onscreen heat between [Nikki and *Alfie*] than with any of the other women [*Alfie*] conquers" (http://movies.about.com/od/alfie/a/alfierev110404.htm).

He not only invites her to live with him, which he has never done before, he also seems to finally have found the right girl. In a scene when Nikki, now dressed in one of his shirts and panties, painting one of his walls blue *Alfie* tells the audience that "she's cracking good in bed", but at the same time when she wants to make love to him he refuses and wants to leave. But she takes the initiative and undresses herself and reveals her naked tiny breasts standing half-nakedly in front of him but *Alfie* still refuses. Walking half-nakedly through his appartment, Nikki takes a cucumber out of the fridge and starts brutally choppong it up into slices as if this cucumber would be *Alfie*'s penis. Here she does not hide her feelings anymore because she is very outraged about his ignoring her. This goes so far that the caring Nikki, who developed housewife qualities, leaves him because she knows she cannot make him stay with her because he used to have more mature women around him. And their relationship does not work out anymore since her demons came out again and she changed to a weird dark person. She is the only of his women, besides Liz, who knows about her sex appeal and uses it for her advantage. But her frankness with being nude does not help her anymore.

II. Masculinity

1. *Alfie* and the minor Characters

This movie mainly focusses on females but nevertheless we find some males here and there. First of all, the protagonist *Alfie*, but also his best friend, Marlon, and their boss, Mr. Wing. We also get to know Julie's new boyfriend, Adam, but since he is a very minor character I will not focus on him but on the other three. What we can find is not only one type of masculinity, we also find a more feminine type of masculinity which we partly find in the characters of Marlon and Mr. Wing.

1.1. *Alfie*

Alfie is a bachelor, working as a chauffeur, who calls himself a "fashin-whore". When we first meet him we find him lying in his bed telling us that he does not take many women home. Interesting to see is what we can find on his table: many condoms, change-mainly coins, stickers with women's addresses and match boxes with women's addresses. So that already tells us that he obviously loves many women and that he is very popular with them. But still, as Joshua Tyler suggests, his "foucus is primarily on himself. He's egotistical, self-sure and as much imagines that his dalliances in some way actually help the women he loves and leaves...he's an unredeemable bastard who uses his smile and charm to get from women what he wants. What he wants is sex with the incredibly beautiful, and lots of it" (http://www.cinemablend.com/reviews/Alfie-714.html). All the women he conquers want him but he cannot simply decide for one only because his motto is "once they seem like they're becoming attached, *Alfie* is quick out the door" (Vince Leo http://qwipster.net/alfie.htm).

Alfie appears to be a tough guy in terms of first getting and then leaving his women but when they leave him we see a hurt *Alfie*. "Women have the power to hurt him, and that's a brand new twist on his free-spirited lifestyle" (Rebecca Murray

9

). When the muscly hunk, *Alfie,* and Dori have sex in the car he can lean back and relax so he does nothing better than talking to the audience. We see that he does not care for Dori because he is in a relationship and needs to get rid of her. The next one on his list is Julie. For her, he is not only the man in the house but also the father to her son. He is not the women-devouring man anymore but a loving father at that point. It seems that Julie is the only one who recognizes his potential for a loving and caring man but she cannot hold him. Not only does she not have all the qualities that *Alfie* wants and needs, but she also does not accept having competition.

That does not go unrecognized for *Alfie*. From this moment on he unconsciously throws himself into romance after romance. The next one who is attracted by *Alfie*'s well-trained body is Lonette. He, according to Desson Thomson, "goes for the moment and ends up sorry. At first, he thinks he's accidently done some good because Lonette immediately reunites with Marlon" but in the end he must find out that he has become a father (). Maybe *Alfie* instinctively thought "[B]lack masculinity [is] a sexual...threat in dominant white cultures" and that is why he hooked up with Lonette; maybe he instinctively did not want Marlon to get her back because he wanted to prove that he can have her as well (R.W. Connell, 254). That is the moment when *Alfie* gets emotional and when he is in his car he cannot help himself anymore and cries endlessly. Something that Susan Brownmiller suggests is a rather feminine quality and therefore unmanly.

> "The catharsis of tears is encouraged in women...Having "a good cry" in order to feel better afterward is not usually recommended as a means of raising the spirits of men... the loss of control was hardly manly" (209).

So here we see that *Alfie* also has a feminine side; he is not only the playboy without feelings he is just to proud to show them.

This emotional cryout is not the only hint that *Alfie* was hurt by women. Julie is the trigger for his unbalanced emotional life; their separation is an emotional burden for Alfie because from that moment on he is impotent and therefore cannot prove his masculinity to Uta and the two lesbians anymore. He equalizes his potency with mortality and from that moment on when he is impotent we can see scenes of a burial taking place, especially when *Alfie* is at the doctor's and looks out of the window. His doctor says his impotency would be caused by emotional stress which *Alfie* leads back to the separation from Julie; so this is the point where he realizes that Julie meant more to him. But as soon as he gets to know that everything is alright after having had a penis biopsy we do not see any more of the burial scenes.

For Nikki and Liz, *Alfie* is not feminine but extremely masculine. *Alfie* seems to be the perfect partner for Nikki; he is the man in the house going to work and earning money and she is the woman behind the stove. He appears to be masculine and smart and tells her what to do, sometimes even roughly. He is much nicer to Liz; he listens to her problems, he cares for her, he loves her and he even wants to propose to her because he thinks she is the right one for him. But she cheats on him and he must realize that he was only one of her toyboys. Now that he realizes that what she has done to him is exactly what he used to do to his girlfriends he gets sentimental and realizes that he could have known before if only he had been able to read between the lines. And here again *Alfie* got hurt by another woman.

1.2. Marlon

Marlon is *Alfie*'s best friend, he is African-American and works as a driver. For Marlon, the male bond to *Alfie* is very important and "seems to be the only person in Alfie's life who isn't there primarily for sexual purposes" (Joshua Tyler http://www.cinemablend.com/reviews/Alfie-714.html). Because they are good friends he wants *Alfie* to help him with Lonette but when they meet again at Marlon's house after seeing the baby Marlon cannot hold his tears back and gets very emotional. He is a feminine type of man because of not holding back his emotions.

> "...a 'man' with a masculine attribute and to understand that attribute as a happy but accidental feature of that man, then it is also possible to speak of a 'man' with a feminine attribute, whatever that is, but still to maintain the integrity of the gender" (Butler 32).

He not only is a man with a female attribute but also soft because he understands *Alfie* when he says he only wanted to help; which in Marlon's eyes is his problem.

1.3. Mr. Wing

Mr. Wing is *Alfie*'s and Marlon's boss and is married to Blossom, who is also Asian-American. We mainly see him as a nitpiking cranky person who tries to be very tough not only with his employeés but also with his wife. He is a bad guy at home and always finds something to argue about with his wife until she leaves him. Suddenly he changes into a crying helpless baby. At that point we see that he is not a real tough guy but a wanna-be who cannot live without his wife. Then he asks *Alfie* for help to get his wife back and he advises him to write a poem for her and give her flowers which Mr. Wing has never done before.

Conclusion

The 2004 version of *Alfie* again presents the protagonist as a lascivious playboy who cannot get enough of women and therefore cannot settle for one. He is capable of every type of women because he knows he can have them all and they cannot resist his charm. Only when he finds the love of his life- a female *Alfie*- he finally realizes what he did wrong in his life. At the same time the movie portrays many different kinds of femininity (a sexually depressed married woman, a beautiful single mom, an African-American girl who dated his best friend, a very frank Hippie girl, two sexually-active lesbians and a rich elderly woman) and masculinity (a tough, smart, cute protagonist playboy and two soft men who uncontrollably cry). *Alfie* clearly knows his priorties and he does not tell his girls about them so they have to find out themselves, which at the end, can be very bitter for them.

Cited Works

Brownmiller, Susan. *Femininity*. New York: Simon & Schuster, 1984.

Butler, Judith. *Gender Trouble*. 1990. New York: Routledge, 1999.

Connell, R.W. "The History of Masculinity." *The Masculinity Sudies Reader*. Eds.: Rachel
    Adams & David Savran. Oxford: Blackwell, 2002.

Grosz, Elizabeth. Space, Time, and Perversion. New York: Routledge, 1995.

Williams, Linda R. *Sex in the Head: Visions of Femininity and Film in H.D. Lawrence*.
    New York, NY [u.a.]: Harvester Wheatsheaf, 1993.

Reviews

Leo, Vince. *Rev of* Alfie, dir. Charles Shyer. Quipster's Movie Review. 2004.
    29. July 2007. <http://qwipster.net/alfie.htm>.

Murray, Rebecca. *Rev of* Alfie, dir. Charles Shyer. About.com: Hollywood Movies. No
    Date. 29. July 2007. <http://movies.about.com/od/alfie/a/alfierev110404.htm> .

Thomson, Desson. *Rev of* 'Alfie': Only A Pretty Face, dir. Charles Shyer. Washington Post
          5 Nov. 2004. 29 July 2007 <http://www.washingtonpost.com/wp-
dyn/content/article/2004/11/05/AR2005033112665.html>.

Tyler, Joshua. *Rev. of* Alfie, dir. Charles Shyer. Cinema Blend 21 Oct. 2004. 29. July 2007.
    <http://www.cinemablend.com/reviews/Alfie-714.html>.